Great Works

Instructional Guide for Literature

The Boy in the Striped Pajamas

A guide for the novel by John Boyne
Great Works Author: Kristin Kemp

SHELL EDUCATION

Publishing Credits

Corinne Burton, M.A.Ed., *President*; Emily R. Smith, M.A.Ed., *Content Director*; Lee Aucoin, *Multimedia Designer*;
Jill K. Mulhall, M.Ed., *Editor*; Stephanie Bernard, *Assistant Editor*; Don Tran, *Production Artist*; Amber Goff, *Editorial Assistant*

Image Credits

Shutterstock (cover)

Standards

© 2007 Teachers of English to Speakers of Other Languages, Inc. (TESOL)
© 2007 Board of Regents of the University of Wisconsin System. World-Class Instructional Design and Assessment (WIDA)
© Copyright 2010. National Governors Association Center for Best Practices and Council of Chief State School Officers.
All rights reserved.

Shell Education

5301 Oceanus Drive
Huntington Beach, CA 92649-1030
http://www.shelleducation.com

ISBN 978-1-4807-8507-6

© 2015 Shell Educational Publishing, Inc.

Printed in USA. WOR004

Table of Contents

How to Use This Literature Guide 4

   Theme Thoughts 4

   Vocabulary 5

   Analyzing the Literature 6

   Reader Response 6

   Close Reading the Literature 6

   Making Connections 7

   Creating with the Story Elements 7

   Culminating Activity 8

   Comprehension Assessment 8

   Response to Literature 8

Correlation to the Standards 8

   Purpose and Intent of Standards 8

   How to Find Standards Correlations 8

   Standards Correlation Chart 9

   TESOL and WIDA Standards 10

About the Author—John Boyne 11

   Possible Texts for Text Comparisons 11

Book Summary of *The Boy in the Striped Pajamas* .12

   Cross-Curricular Connection 12

   Possible Texts for Text Sets 12

Teacher Plans and Student Pages 13

   Pre-Reading Theme Thoughts 13

   Section 1: Chapters 1-4 14

   Section 2: Chapters 5-7 24

   Section 3: Chapters 8-11 34

   Section 4: Chapters 12-15 44

   Section 5: Chapters 16-20 54

Post-Reading Activities 64

   Post-Reading Theme Thoughts 64

   Culminating Activity: Book Review 65

   Comprehension Assessment 67

   Response to Literature: Modern-Day Fences 69

Answer Key 71

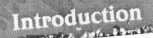
How to Use This Literature Guide

Today's standards demand rigor and relevance in the reading of complex texts. The units in this series guide teachers in a rich and deep exploration of worthwhile works of literature for classroom study. The most rigorous instruction can also be interesting and engaging!

Many current strategies for effective literacy instruction have been incorporated into these instructional guides for literature. Throughout the units, text-dependent questions are used to determine comprehension of the book as well as student interpretation of the vocabulary words. The books chosen for the series are complex exemplars of carefully crafted works of literature. Close reading is used throughout the units to guide students toward revisiting the text and using textual evidence to respond to prompts orally and in writing. Students must analyze the story elements in multiple assignments for each section of the book. All of these strategies work together to rigorously guide students through their study of literature.

The next few pages will make clear how to use this guide for a purposeful and meaningful literature study. Each section of this guide is set up in the same way to make it easier for you to implement the instruction in your classroom.

Theme Thoughts

The great works of literature used throughout this series have important themes that have been relevant to people for many years. Many of the themes will be discussed during the various sections of this instructional guide. However, it would also benefit students to have independent time to think about the key themes of the novel.

Before students begin reading, have them complete *Pre-Reading Theme Thoughts* (page 13). This graphic organizer will allow students to think about the themes outside the context of the story. They'll have the opportunity to evaluate statements based on important themes and defend their opinions. Be sure to have students keep their papers for comparison to the *Post-Reading Theme Thoughts* (page 64). This graphic organizer is similar to the pre-reading activity. However, this time, students will be answering the questions from the point of view of one of the characters in the novel. They have to think about how the character would feel about each statement and defend their thoughts. To conclude the activity, have students compare what they thought about the themes before they read the novel to what the characters discovered during the story.

How to Use This Literature Guide (cont.)

Vocabulary

Each teacher overview page has definitions and sentences about how key vocabulary words are used in the section. These words should be introduced and discussed with students. There are two student vocabulary activity pages in each section. On the first page, students are asked to define the ten words chosen by the author of this unit. On the second page in most sections, each student will select at least eight words that he or she finds interesting or difficult. For each section, choose one of these pages for your students to complete. With either assignment, you may want to have students get into pairs to discuss the meanings of the words. Allow students to use reference guides to define the words. Monitor students to make sure the definitions they have found are accurate and relate to how the words are used in the text.

On some of the vocabulary student pages, students are asked to answer text-related questions about the vocabulary words. The following question stems will help you create your own vocabulary questions if you'd like to extend the discussion.

- How does this word describe _____'s character?
- In what ways does this word relate to the problem in this story?
- How does this word help you understand the setting?
- In what ways is this word related to the story's solution?
- Describe how this word supports the novel's theme of . . . .
- What visual images does this word bring to your mind?
- For what reasons might the author have chosen to use this particular word?

At times, more work with the words will help students understand their meanings. The following quick vocabulary activities are a good way to further study the words.

- Have students practice their vocabulary and writing skills by creating sentences and/or paragraphs in which multiple vocabulary words are used correctly and with evidence of understanding.
- Students can play vocabulary concentration. Students make a set of cards with the words and a separate set of cards with the definitions. Then, students lay the cards out on the table and play concentration. The goal of the game is to match vocabulary words with their definitions.
- Students can create word journal entries about the words. Students choose words they think are important and then describe why they think each word is important within the novel.

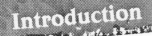
How to Use This Literature Guide (cont.)

Analyzing the Literature

After students have read each section, hold small-group or whole-class discussions. Questions are written at two levels of complexity to allow you to decide which questions best meet the needs of your students. The Level 1 questions are typically less abstract than the Level 2 questions. Level 1 is indicated by a square, while Level 2 is indicated by a triangle. These questions focus on the various story elements, such as character, setting, and plot. Student pages are provided if you want to assign these questions for individual student work before your group discussion. Be sure to add further questions as your students discuss what they've read. For each question, a few key points are provided for your reference as you discuss the novel with students.

Reader Response

In today's classrooms, there are often great readers who are below-average writers. So much time and energy is spent in classrooms getting students to read on grade level that little time is left to focus on writing skills. To help teachers include more writing in their daily literacy instruction, each section of this guide has a literature-based reader response prompt. Each of the three genres of writing is used in the reader responses within this guide: narrative, informative/explanatory, and opinion/argument. Students have a choice between two prompts for each reader response. One response requires students to make connections between the reading and their own lives. The other prompt requires students to determine text-to-text connections or connections within the text.

Close Reading the Literature

Within each section, students are asked to closely reread a short section of text. Since some versions of the novels have different page numbers, the selections are described by chapter and location, along with quotations to guide the readers. After each close reading, there are text-dependent questions to be answered by students.

Encourage students to read each question one at a time and then go back to the text and discover the answer. Work with students to ensure that they use the text to determine their answers rather than making unsupported inferences. Once students have answered the questions, discuss what they discovered. Suggested answers are provided in the answer key.

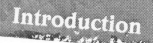

How to Use This Literature Guide (cont.)

Close Reading the Literature (cont.)

The generic, open-ended stems below can be used to write your own text-dependent questions if you would like to give students more practice.

- Give evidence from the text to support . . . .
- Justify your thinking using text evidence about . . . .
- Find evidence to support your conclusions about . . . .
- What text evidence helps the reader understand . . . ?
- Use the book to tell why _____ happens.
- Based on events in the story, ...
- Use text evidence to describe why . . . .

Making Connections

The activities in this section help students make cross-curricular connections to writing, mathematics, science, social studies, or the fine arts. Each of these types of activities requires higher-order thinking skills from students.

Creating with the Story Elements

It is important to spend time discussing the common story elements in literature. Understanding the characters, setting, and plot can increase students' comprehension and appreciation of the story. If teachers discuss these elements daily, students will more likely internalize the concepts and look for the elements in their independent reading. Another important reason for focusing on the story elements is that students will be better writers if they think about how the stories they read are constructed.

Students are given three options for working with the story elements. They are asked to create something related to the characters, setting, or plot of the novel. Students are given a choice in this activity so that they can decide to complete the activity that most appeals to them. Different multiple intelligences are used so that the activities are diverse and interesting to all students.

How to Use This Literature Guide *(cont.)*

Culminating Activity

This open-ended, cross-curricular activity requires higher-order thinking and allows for a creative product. Students will enjoy getting the chance to share what they have discovered through reading the novel. Be sure to allow them enough time to complete the activity at school or home.

Comprehension Assessment

The questions in this section are modeled after current standardized tests to help students analyze what they've read and prepare for tests they may see in their classrooms. The questions are dependent on the text and require critical-thinking skills to answer.

Response to Literature

The final post-reading activity is an essay based on the text that also requires further research by students. This is a great way to extend this book into other curricular areas. A suggested rubric is provided for teacher reference.

Correlation to the Standards

Shell Education is committed to producing educational materials that are research and standards based. As part of this effort, we have correlated all of our products to the academic standards of all 50 states, the District of Columbia, the Department of Defense Dependents Schools, and all Canadian provinces.

Purpose and Intent of Standards

Standards are designed to focus instruction and guide adoption of curricula. Standards are statements that describe the criteria necessary for students to meet specific academic goals. They define the knowledge, skills, and content students should acquire at each level. Standards are also used to develop standardized tests to evaluate students' academic progress. Teachers are required to demonstrate how their lessons meet standards. Standards are used in the development of all of our products, so educators can be assured they meet high academic standards.

How to Find Standards Correlations

To print a customized correlation report of this product for your state, visit our website at http://www.shelleducation.com and follow the online directions. If you require assistance in printing correlation reports, please contact our Customer Service Department at 1-877-777-3450.

Correlation to the Standards (cont.)

Standards Correlation Chart

The lessons in this guide were written to support today's college and career readiness standards. This chart indicates which sections of this guide address which standards.

College and Career Readiness Standards	Section
Read closely to determine what the text says explicitly and to make logical inferences from it; cite specific textual evidence when writing or speaking to support conclusions drawn from the text. (R.1)	Analyzing the Literature Sections 1–5; Close Reading the Literature Sections 1–5; Making Connections Sections 1, 5; Post-Reading Response to Literature
Determine central ideas or themes of a text and analyze their development; summarize the key supporting details and ideas. (R.2)	Analyzing the Literature Sections 1–5; Making Connections Section 4
Analyze how and why individuals, events, or ideas develop and interact over the course of a text. (R.3)	Analyzing the Literature Sections 1–5; Making Connections Section 3
Interpret words and phrases as they are used in a text, including determining technical, connotative, and figurative meanings, and analyze how specific word choices shape meaning or tone. (R.4)	Vocabulary Sections 1–5
Read and comprehend complex literary and informational texts independently and proficiently. (R.10)	Entire Unit
Write arguments to support claims in an analysis of substantive topics or texts using valid reasoning and relevant and sufficient evidence. (W.1)	Analyzing the Literature Sections 1–5; Close Reading the Literature Sections 1–5; Reader Response Sections 2–5; Making Connections Sections 2, 5
Write informative/explanatory texts to examine and convey complex ideas and information clearly and accurately through the effective selection, organization, and analysis of content. (W.2)	Reader Response Sections 1–2, 4–5; Post-Reading Response to Literature
Write narratives to develop real or imagined experiences or events using effective technique, well-chosen details and well-structured event sequences. (W.3)	Reader Response Sections 1, 3; Creating with the Story Elements Sections 1–5
Produce clear and coherent writing in which the development, organization, and style are appropriate to task, purpose, and audience. (W.4)	Reader Response Sections 1–5; Culminating Activity; Post-Reading Response to Literature
Develop and strengthen writing as needed by planning, revising, editing, rewriting, or trying a new approach. (W.5)	Culminating Activity; Post-Reading Response to Literature
Use technology, including the Internet, to produce and publish writing and to interact and collaborate with others. (W.6)	Culminating Activity

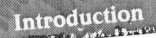

Correlation to the Standards (cont.)

Standards Correlation Chart (cont.)

College and Career Readiness Standards	Section
Conduct short as well as more sustained research projects based on focused questions, demonstrating understanding of the subject under investigation. (W.7)	Analyzing the Literature Sections 1–5; Reader Response Sections 1–5; Post-Reading Response to Literature
Write routinely over extended time frames (time for research, reflection, and revision) and shorter time frames (a single sitting or a day or two) for a range of tasks, purposes, and audiences. (W.10)	Reader Response Sections 1–5; Post-Reading Response to Literature
Make strategic use of digital media and visual displays of data to express information and enhance understanding of presentations. (SL.5)	Culminating Activity
Adapt speech to a variety of contexts and communicative tasks, demonstrating command of formal English when indicated or appropriate. (SL.6)	Culminating Activity
Demonstrate command of the conventions of standard English grammar and usage when writing or speaking. (L.1)	Entire Unit
Demonstrate command of the conventions of standard English capitalization, punctuation, and spelling when writing. (L.2)	Entire Unit
Determine or clarify the meaning of unknown and multiple-meaning words and phrases by using context clues, analyzing meaningful word parts, and consulting general and specialized reference materials, as appropriate. (L.4)	Vocabulary Sections 1–5
Acquire and use accurately a range of general academic and domain-specific words and phrases sufficient for reading, writing, speaking, and listening at the college and career readiness level; demonstrate independence in gathering vocabulary knowledge when encountering an unknown term important to comprehension or expression. (L.6)	Vocabulary Sections 1–5

TESOL and WIDA Standards

The lessons in this book promote English language development for English language learners. The following TESOL and WIDA English Language Development Standards are addressed through the activities in this book:

- Standard 1: English language learners communicate for social and instructional purposes within the school setting.

- Standard 2: English language learners communicate information, ideas and concepts necessary for academic success in the content area of language arts.

About the Author—John Boyne

John Boyne was born in Dublin, Ireland, in 1971. He knew from childhood that he would be an author. Surrounded by books in his home and a frequent visitor to the library, Boyne began creating his own stories when he was 10 or 11 years old, complete with binding and his name on the spine. C. S. Lewis's *Chronicles of Narnia* series and the "orphan boy" books by Charles Dickens were early influences. He enjoyed adventure stories and reading about young characters who got themselves out of trouble by solving problems on their own.

Boyne studied English literature at Trinity College in Dublin and creative writing at the University of East Anglia in Norwich. At the beginning of his career, he mostly wrote short stories, many of which were published in magazines or anthologies. His first novel, *The Thief of Time*, was published in 2000.

As of 2014, Boyne has published nine novels for adults, four novels for younger readers, and more than 70 short stories. His books have been published in 47 languages and have received much acclaim. In 2012, Boyne was awarded the Hennessy Literary Hall of Fame Award for his body of work. He has also received three Irish Book Awards.

Boyne's best-known work is the novel for young readers, *The Boy in the Striped Pajamas*, which was published in 2006. The novel reached number one on *The New York Times* Bestseller's list, has sold more than six million copies worldwide, and was made into a major motion picture in 2008.

The author says that *The Boy in the Striped Pajamas* started with a simple image in his mind: two boys sitting on opposite sides of a fence, having a conversation. He wrote the book in a very short period of time, almost without stopping, which is unusual for him. According to Boyne, he felt that the voice of the book "took over" his writing, and he worried that if he stopped writing, he would lose it.

While some question Boyne's decision to have Bruno, the young character at the center of *The Boy in the Striped Pajamas*, be so ignorant and naïve about the events at "Out-With," Boyne maintains he felt it was the only way he could respectfully deal with something as horrible as the Holocaust. "After all," he wrote in the novel's author's note, "only the victims and survivors can truly comprehend the awfulness of that time and place; the rest of us live on the other side of the fence."

Boyne resides in Dublin with his dog and continues to pursue his lifelong passion of writing. Check out John Boyne's website at **http://www.johnboyne.com**.

Possible Texts for Text Comparisons

Other books for younger readers by Boyne include: *Noah Barleywater Runs Away*, *The Terrible Thing that Happened to Barnaby Brocket*, and *Stay Where You Are and Then Leave*. Though the books' topics vary, they all deal with young boys facing social or emotional obstacles.

Book Summary of *The Boy in the Striped Pajamas*

Nine-year-old Bruno enjoys his life in World War II-era Berlin, Germany. He has a house with five stories and many places to explore, three best friends for life, and a military leader father who wears an impressive uniform and shiny boots. All of this changes when his father receives a promotion from the government's leader, "the Fury," and the family moves to a smaller home far from his friends. Bruno learns his new home, where he is miserable, is called "Out-With." From his window, he can see a tall fence and a camp of people, all boys and men, who wear striped pajamas and hats every day.

During one of his outdoor explorations, Bruno meets a boy from the other side of the fence, Shmuel. Over the course of a year, the boys forge a friendship as they have daily conversations through the fence. Bruno sometimes brings snacks for Shmuel and they talk about their families and lives. Bruno wonders at the strangeness of Shmuel's situation—why he is so thin and seems so sad, why he is living at the camp, and why he sometimes shows up with bruises on his body.

Though in many ways Bruno remains blissfully naïve, other characters lend clarification to the events at hand. Maria, the family's maid, confides that though Bruno's father is a good man, she cannot understand why he is involved in Out-With. Lieutenant Kotler, a young soldier often at Bruno's house, displays hatred and prejudice. Pavel, the gentle and educated waiter for Bruno's family, is revealed to be a resident at the camp who is brought to the house to work for the family.

When Shmuel's father goes missing, Bruno agrees to help look for him inside the camp. The day Bruno crawls under the fence changes his family forever.

Cross-Curricular Connection

This book could be used during a social studies unit on World War II and the Holocaust or a unit on social discrimination and prejudice.

Possible Texts for Text Sets

- Callery, Sean. *Scholastic Discover More: World War II*. Scholastic Reference, 2013.
- Dauvillier, Loic, and Greg Salsedo. *Hidden: A Child's Story of the Holocaust*. First Second, 2014.
- Frank, Anne. *Anne Frank: The Diary of a Young Girl*. Bantam, 1993.
- Zullo, Allan. *Survivors: True Stories of Children in the Holocaust*. Scholastic Paperbacks, 2005.
- Zusak, Markus. *The Book Thief*. Alfred A. Knopf, 2007.

Name ....

Date ....

Pre-Reading Theme Thoughts

Directions: Read each of the statements in the first column. Decide if you agree or disagree with the statements. Record your opinion by marking an X in Agree or Disagree for each statement. Explain your choices in the fourth column. There are no right or wrong answers.

Statement	Agree	Disagree	Explain Your Answer
It is best to protect children from knowing about difficult things.			
A person should always support his or her family members.			
If a person is doing something wrong, he or she knows it.			
People who are very different can be friends.			

Vocabulary Overview

Ten key words from this section are provided below with definitions and sentences about how the words are used in the book. Choose one of the vocabulary activity sheets (pages 15 or 16) for students to complete as they read this section. Monitor students as they work to ensure the definitions they have found are accurate and relate to the text. Finally, discuss these important vocabulary words with students. If you think these words or other words in the section warrant more time devoted to them, there are suggestions in the introduction for other vocabulary activities (page 5).

Word	Definition	Sentence about Text
muster (ch. 1)	summon; gather	Bruno speaks to Maria in as nice of a tone as he can **muster**.
presumed (ch. 1)	assumed that something was true without knowing for sure	Bruno **presumes** his grandparents are coming with his family to the new job.
desolate (ch. 2)	empty or bare; without anything welcoming	The new house stands in a **desolate** place with no other houses nearby.
foreseeable (ch. 2)	able to be predicted	Mother tells Bruno this is their new home for the **foreseeable** future.
priorities (ch. 2)	things considered more important than others	Bruno feels Maria, who has unpacked his clothes before his toys, does not have her **priorities** right.
resigned (ch. 3)	accepted something; realized you cannot do anything about something	Bruno **resigns** himself to staying at the new house for a month.
acknowledging (ch. 3)	accepting; admitting that something is true	Gretel **acknowledges** Bruno's comment that the new house is horrible right now.
moor (ch. 4)	an open area of wasteland, often overgrown	Building a beautiful garden next to an ugly, desolate house is like lighting one small candle in a huge castle that sits on a dark, misty **moor**.
conviction (ch. 4)	a firmly held opinion	Sure that Gretel is wrong, Bruno shakes his head and speaks with **conviction**.
decidedly (ch. 4)	without doubt; undeniably	Gretel thinks the view is **decidedly** better from the window in her room.

Name

Date

Understanding Vocabulary Words

Directions: The following words appear in this section of the book. Use context clues and reference materials to determine an accurate definition for each word.

Word	Definition
muster (ch. 1)	
presumed (ch. 1)	
desolate (ch. 2)	
foreseeable (ch. 2)	
priorities (ch. 2)	
resigned (ch. 3)	
acknowledging (ch. 3)	
moor (ch. 4)	
conviction (ch. 4)	
decidedly (ch. 4)	

Name _____

Date _____

During-Reading Vocabulary Activity

Directions: As you read these chapters, record at least eight important words on the lines below. Try to find interesting, difficult, intriguing, special, or funny words. Your words can be long or short. They can be hard or easy to spell. After each word, use context clues in the text and reference materials to define the word.

- _____
- _____
- _____
- _____
- _____
- _____
- _____
- _____
- _____
- _____

Directions: Respond to these questions about the words in this section.

1. What **priorities** does Bruno feel Maria should have?

_____

_____

2. Why does Gretel feel her view is **decidedly** better than Bruno's?

_____

_____

Analyzing the Literature

Provided below are discussion questions you can use in small groups, with the whole class, or for written assignments. Each question is given at two levels so you can choose the right question for each group of students. Activity sheets with these questions are provided (pages 18–19) if you want students to write their responses. For each question, a few key discussion points are provided for your reference.

Story Element	■ Level 1	▲ Level 2	Key Discussion Points
Plot	Why does Bruno's family move?	How do the different characters feel about moving away from Berlin?	Bruno's family moves because his father has a high rank in the military and has been given a new position at Out-With. Bruno, Gretel, his mother, and Maria are all unhappy about the move. Bruno and Gretel are outspoken about their unhappiness, but Mother and Maria tell Bruno it is for the best and they must follow Father to his new position.
Setting	What does Bruno enjoy about his home in Berlin?	Compare and contrast Bruno's home in Berlin to his new home at Out-With.	Bruno loves that his house has five floors and has plenty of places for him to explore. It has a banister he can slide down and is close to the market, his friends, and his grandparents. The new home is much smaller, with only three floors, and is in the middle of nowhere. There are no neighbors or market carts nearby and soldiers are in his house all of the time.
Character	Who is Maria and what does she do for Bruno's family?	Describe Bruno's relationship with Maria.	Maria is the family's maid. She takes care of their home and packs/unpacks for Bruno during the move. Bruno treats and speaks to Maria like a servant, but he also has a candid relationship with her and talks with her about things he cannot discuss with his parents.
Plot	Describe the view from Bruno's window.	What are Bruno's and Gretel's reactions to what they see outside Bruno's window?	Outside Bruno's window, there is a garden. Beyond that, there is a tall, long fence with barbed wire around the top. He can see small huts and hundreds of people—all male—walking around. Neither Bruno nor Gretel like the camp. They feel it is dirty and the people are not ones with whom they would be friends. They struggle to make sense of what they see. Gretel thinks it may be the countryside, but they decide it is not.

Name _____

Date _____

■ Analyzing the Literature

Directions: Think about the section you just read. Read each question and state your response with textual evidence.

1. Why does Bruno's family move?

_____

_____

_____

_____

2. What does Bruno enjoy about his home in Berlin?

_____

_____

_____

_____

3. Who is Maria and what does she do for Bruno's family?

_____

_____

_____

_____

4. Describe the view from Bruno's window.

_____

_____

_____

_____

Name _____

Date _____

▲ Analyzing the Literature

Directions: Think about the section you just read. Read each question and state your response with textual evidence.

1. How do the different characters feel about moving away from Berlin?

_____

_____

_____

_____

2. Compare and contrast Bruno's home in Berlin to his new home at Out-With.

_____

_____

_____

_____

3. Describe Bruno's relationship with Maria.

_____

_____

_____

_____

4. What are Bruno's and Gretel's reactions to what they see outside Bruno's window?

_____

_____

_____

_____

Name _____

Date _____

Reader Response

Directions: Choose one of the following prompts about this section to answer. Be sure you include a topic sentence in your response, use textual evidence to support your opinion, and provide a strong conclusion that summarizes your opinion.

Writing Prompts

- **Narrative Piece**—Moving to Out-With is a big change for Bruno. Write about a time you or your family experienced a big change.
- **Informative/Explanatory Piece**—Write at least two questions you have about Out-With so far. Explain why you are curious to find out the answers.

_____

_____

_____

_____

_____

_____

_____

_____

_____

_____

_____

_____

_____

_____

_____

_____

Name _____

Date _____

Close Reading the Literature

Directions: Closely reread the section in chapter 4 when Gretel and Bruno discuss the countryside. Begin when Gretel says, "This must be the countryside." Read until she says, "And what are they all doing there?" Read each question below, and then revisit the text to find evidence that supports your answer.

1. Why does Gretel suggest that they are at the countryside?

   _____

   _____

   _____

2. When Bruno first disagrees with Gretel, how does she respond?

   _____

   _____

   _____

3. Use the text to describe Bruno's reasons for arguing that they cannot be at the countryside.

   _____

   _____

   _____

4. What does Bruno wish, for just a moment, when he sits down on the bed?

   _____

   _____

   _____

Name _____

Date _____

Making Connections—World War II Timeline

Directions: Read this World War II timeline. Then, answer the questions below.

1934—August	Hitler becomes leader, or Führer, of Germany
1939—September	Britain and France (the Allies) declare war on Germany
1940—September	Germany, Italy, and Japan sign a pact and become the Axis Alliance
1941—December	Japan bombs Pearl Harbor in Hawaii; the United States joins the Allies and enters the war
1944—June	The Allies invade Normandy, France, in a big attack called D-Day; the Allies win and take the land from the Germans
1944—December	Germany leads a surprise attack on the Allies called the Battle of the Bulge; the Allies win
1945—May	Germany surrenders to the Allies
1945—August	United States drops atomic bombs on Hiroshima and Nagasaki, Japan; Japan surrenders to the Allies

1. For how many years did the Allies fight before the United States joined?

   _____

2. What event caused the United States to join the Allies?

   _____

3. List two major victories for the Allies.

   _____

4. Why do you think countries join together during wars to form groups like the Allies and the Axis Alliance?

   _____

   _____

   _____

Name _____

Date _____

Creating with the Story Elements

Directions: Thinking about the story elements of character, setting, and plot in a novel is very important to understanding what is happening and why. Complete **one** of the following activities based on what you've read so far. Be creative and have fun!

Characters

Think of at least three words or phrases that describe Bruno. Find a quotation or sentence in the book that supports each description.

Setting

Create a "For Sale" brochure for Bruno's new home at Out-With. Include an illustration and description of the house, as well as the surrounding area. Use details from the book as well as your imagination.

Plot

Write a letter from Bruno to one of his friends in Berlin describing the move, how he is feeling, and what he has discovered at Out-With.

Vocabulary Overview

Ten key words from this section are provided below with definitions and sentences about how the words are used in the book. Choose one of the vocabulary activity sheets (pages 25 or 26) for students to complete as they read this section. Monitor students as they work to ensure the definitions they have found are accurate and relate to the text. Finally, discuss these important vocabulary words with students. If you think these words or other words in the section warrant more time devoted to them, there are suggestions in the introduction for other vocabulary activities (page 5).

Word	Definition	Sentence about Text
efficiency (ch. 5)	doing something without wasting time, energy, or materials	The soldiers feel that, under the previous leader, the camp lacked **efficiency**.
complementing (ch. 5)	something that completes something else or makes it better	Mother and Grandmother give many hugs, then **complement** them with kisses.
ergo (ch. 5)	therefore; for that reason	Bruno's family is at Out-With, **ergo**, it must be their home.
insolent (ch. 5)	rude or disrespectful	Bruno's father is upset when he thinks that Bruno is speaking to him in an **insolent** manner.
deliberately (ch. 6)	on purpose; intentionally	Maria chooses her words carefully, which Bruno misunderstands as being **deliberately** difficult.
peckish (ch. 6)	slightly hungry	Bruno feels **peckish** during his conversation with Maria.
incredulous (ch. 6)	unable to believe something	Bruno is **incredulous** when Maria tells him that he is not allowed to talk about his feelings.
escapade (ch. 7)	a foolish or dangerous experience	Mother says Bruno shouldn't laugh at poor Herr Roller's latest **escapade**.
diversion (ch. 7)	an activity created to pass the time	To keep himself entertained one Saturday, Bruno creates a **diversion** for himself.
appallingly (ch. 7)	something bad in a way that causes fear, shock, or disgust	Lieutenant Kotler ruffles Bruno's hair, a gesture that Bruno finds quite **appalling**.

Name _____

Date _____

Understanding Vocabulary Words

Directions: The following words appear in this section of the book. Use context clues and reference materials to determine an accurate definition for each word.

Word	Definition
efficiency (ch. 5)	
complementing (ch. 5)	
ergo (ch. 5)	
insolent (ch. 5)	
deliberately (ch. 6)	
peckish (ch. 6)	
incredulous (ch. 6)	
escapade (ch. 7)	
diversion (ch. 7)	
appallingly (ch. 7)	

Name _____

Date _____

During-Reading Vocabulary Activity

Directions: As you read these chapters, record at least eight important words on the lines below. Try to find interesting, difficult, intriguing, special, or funny words. Your words can be long or short. They can be hard or easy to spell. After each word, use context clues in the text and reference materials to define the word.

- _____
- _____
- _____
- _____
- _____
- _____
- _____
- _____
- _____
- _____
- _____

Directions: Respond to these questions about the words in this section.

1. What statement makes Bruno feel **incredulous** while speaking with Maria?

   _____

   _____

2. According to Mother, why should Bruno not laugh at Herr Roller's **escapades**?

   _____

   _____

Analyzing the Literature

Provided below are discussion questions you can use in small groups, with the whole class, or for written assignments. Each question is given at two levels so you can choose the right question for each group of students. Activity sheets with these questions are provided (pages 28–29) if you want students to write their responses. For each question, a few key discussion points are provided for your reference.

Story Element	■ Level 1	▲ Level 2	Key Discussion Points
Character	How does Bruno feel about his father?	What clues in the text show that Bruno admires his father?	Bruno is proud of his father and admires him very much. He may feel a bit intimidated by him and is obedient to him. Textual clues include: Bruno feels Father's voice carries better and his uniform and hair are nicer than anyone else's; the other soldiers want Father's attention and they are quiet the moment Father raises his hands.
Character	How did Maria get her job as Bruno's family's maid?	What does Maria's story about getting her job with Bruno's family reveal about Father's character?	Maria's mother worked for Father's mother. He gave Maria a job because she was poor and hungry. When Maria's mother became ill and died, Father paid for her medicine and funeral. This shows he is compassionate, loyal, and takes care of others even when he is not obligated.
Character	What examples from the text show that Bruno does not like Lieutenant Kotler?	What is the significance of Gretel feeling uncomfortable when Lieutenant Kotler shouts at Pavel?	The text says Kotler makes Bruno feel cold. Bruno complains Kotler wears too much cologne, calls him "little man," and ruffles Bruno's hair as though he is a small child. When Kotler shouts at Pavel and calls him a name, it is so hateful it makes even Gretel uncomfortable. Earlier, she had been admiring Kotler, but her reaction shows how derogatory his comment is.
Plot	Why is Bruno upset that Mother will tell Father she cleaned up Bruno?	Why does Mother say that they will tell Father that she treated Bruno's injury?	Bruno is upset because he feels his mother will be taking credit for something heroic she did not do. Mother does this because Pavel is Jewish and lives at the camp. She knows Father would disapprove of his help in such a personal and physical matter.

Name _____

Date _____

■ Analyzing the Literature

Directions: Think about the section you just read. Read each question and state your response with textual evidence.

1. How does Bruno feel about his father?

_____

_____

_____

_____

2. How did Maria get her job as Bruno's family's maid?

_____

_____

_____

_____

3. What examples from the text show that Bruno does not like Lieutenant Kotler?

_____

_____

_____

_____

4. Why is Bruno upset that Mother will tell Father she cleaned up Bruno?

_____

_____

_____

_____

▲ Analyzing the Literature

Directions: Think about the section you just read. Read each question and state your response with textual evidence.

1. What clues in the text show that Bruno admires his father?

_____

_____

_____

_____

2. What does Maria's story about getting her job with Bruno's family reveal about Father's character?

_____

_____

_____

_____

3. What is the significance of Gretel feeling uncomfortable when Lieutenant Kotler shouts at Pavel?

_____

_____

_____

_____

4. Why does Mother say that they will tell Father that she treated Bruno's injury?

_____

_____

_____

Name

Date

Reader Response

Directions: Choose one of the following prompts about this section to answer. Be sure you include a topic sentence in your response, use textual evidence to support your opinion, and provide a strong conclusion that summarizes your opinion.

Writing Prompts

- **Informative/Explanatory Piece**—Maria is a trusted adult, not related to Bruno, with whom he can have honest conversations. Describe the adults who fulfill this role for you.
- **Opinion/Argument Piece**—Explain whether you think Bruno is being brave or disrespectful during his conversation with Father in his office. Include examples to support your opinion.

_____

_____

_____

_____

_____

_____

_____

_____

_____

_____

_____

_____

_____

Name _____

Date _____

Close Reading the Literature

Directions: Closely reread the section after Pavel treats Bruno's wound in chapter 7. Begin when Bruno says, "Well, how do you know?" Read to the end of the chapter. Read each question below, and then revisit the text to find evidence that supports your answer.

1. According to the text, why is Bruno surprised to find out Pavel is a doctor?

   _____

   _____

   _____

2. What is the misunderstanding between Bruno and Pavel about the phrase, "practised as a doctor?" Use context clues to explain your answer.

   _____

   _____

   _____

3. What can you infer from Pavel saying, "I think I've always been here" to Bruno? Use evidence from the text to support your ideas.

   _____

   _____

   _____

4. How does Pavel react when Mother's voice is overheard outside?

   _____

   _____

   _____

Name _____

Date _____

Making Connections–Make a Tire Swing

Directions: Bruno builds a tire swing as a diversion on a long Saturday. Describe how to build a tire swing the way Bruno does it, in four steps. Illustrate each step in the box next to it. Then, answer the question below.

1. _____

   _____

   _____

2. _____

   _____

   _____

3. _____

   _____

   _____

4. _____

   _____

   _____

Do you think children should build tire swings by themselves? Give at least two reasons to support your answer.

_____

_____

_____

_____

Name _____

Date _____

Creating with the Story Elements

Directions: Thinking about the story elements of character, setting, and plot in a novel is very important to understanding what is happening and why. Complete **one** of the following activities based on what you've read so far. Be creative and have fun!

Characters

Create a Venn diagram to compare and contrast Father and Lieutenant Kotler. Include at least four ideas for each individual character and at least three ideas for things they have in common.

Setting

Draw a picture of Father's office. Use details from the text and your imagination.

Plot

Pretend you are writing up the medical paperwork on Bruno's injury for a doctor or hospital. Include how the injury occurred, how it was treated, and how it should be cared for as it heals.

Vocabulary Overview

Ten key words from this section are provided below with definitions and sentences about how the words are used in the book. Choose one of the vocabulary activity sheets (pages 35 or 36) for students to complete as they read this section. Monitor students as they work to ensure the definitions they have found are accurate and relate to the text. Finally, discuss these important vocabulary words with students. If you think these words or other words in the section warrant more time devoted to them, there are suggestions in the introduction for other vocabulary activities (page 5).

Word	Definition	Sentence about Text
dominated (ch. 8)	was the most important part; controlled	Parties at Bruno's house are **dominated** by his Grandmother's singing.
coincide (ch. 8)	happen at the same time	Funnily, Grandmother's singing always seems to **coincide** with Mother leaving the room.
devise (ch. 8)	to plan with careful thought	Every Christmas and birthday, Grandmother **devises** a play for the children to perform with her.
reclaim (ch. 8)	to get back something that was lost or taken away	Grandfather thinks Father, with his important position, is helping Germany **reclaim** her pride.
boneshaker (ch. 9)	an old-fashioned bicycle with solid tires and no springs	Bruno's tutor, Herr Liszt, rattles up to the house on his old **boneshaker**.
sinister (ch. 9)	hinting of something bad or evil	Herr Liszt speaks in a **sinister** voice when he says he will change what Bruno reads.
forlorn (ch. 10)	very sad or lonely	The boy on the other side of the fence sits on the ground with a **forlorn** expression on his face.
resolution (ch. 10)	a firm decision to do (or not to do) something	Bruno makes a private **resolution** to pay more attention during his geography lessons.
nonetheless (ch. 11)	in spite of; however	Gretel is told not to call Bruno stupid, but she sticks out her tongue at him **nonetheless**.
enunciating (ch. 11)	carefully pronouncing	Father wants the children to speak clearly, **enunciating** every word.

Name _____

Date _____

Understanding Vocabulary Words

Directions: The following words appear in this section of the book. Use context clues and reference materials to determine an accurate definition for each word.

Word	Definition
dominated (ch. 8)	
coincide (ch. 8)	
devise (ch. 8)	
reclaim (ch. 8)	
boneshaker (ch. 9)	
sinister (ch. 9)	
forlorn (ch. 10)	
resolution (ch. 10)	
nonetheless (ch. 11)	
enunciating (ch. 11)	

Name _____

Date _____

During-Reading Vocabulary Activity

Directions: As you read these chapters, record at least eight important words on the lines below. Try to find interesting, difficult, intriguing, special, or funny words. Your words can be long or short. They can be hard or easy to spell. After each word, use context clues in the text and reference materials to define the word.

- _____

- _____

- _____

- _____

- _____

- _____

- _____

- _____

- _____

- _____

Directions: Now, organize your words. Rewrite each of your words on a sticky note. Work as a group to create a bar graph of your words. You should stack any words that are the same on top of one another. Different words appear in different columns. Finally, discuss with a group why certain words were chosen more often than other words.

Analyzing the Literature

Provided below are discussion questions you can use in small groups, with the whole class, or for written assignments. Each question is given at two levels so you can choose the right question for each group of students. Activity sheets with these questions are provided (pages 38–39) if you want students to write their responses. For each question, a few key discussion points are provided for your reference.

Story Element	■ Level 1	▲ Level 2	Key Discussion Points
Plot	Why does Bruno's family argue on Christmas day?	How does the argument on Christmas illustrate differing opinions in Germany at the time?	Bruno's grandmother does not approve of Father's position in the military or what he is doing (working for and supporting "the Fury"). Bruno's grandfather is very proud of his son and thinks he will help restore Germany back to its deserved glory. These differing opinions echo those of others during the time.
Setting	Why does Bruno decide to explore outside at Out-With instead of inside like in Berlin?	Why is Bruno so curious about the fence and the people who live behind it?	Bruno's home at Out-With is much smaller without the nooks and crannies of his house in Berlin. He also realizes he knows very little about the people in the striped pajamas. He is curious why they are there and what they do. He sees men in uniform and striped pajamas mixing company occasionally, but he wonders who decides which men wear which clothes and why the uniformed men are the ones in charge.
Character	Use the text to describe Shmuel.	Compare and contrast Bruno and Shmuel.	Shmuel is very skinny and sad with a forlorn look in his eyes. He is also educated, as he can speak both German and Polish. Bruno, though tutored, does not seem as serious about schooling. Both boys have the same birthday and seem eager to be friends. They both state their own opinions and disagree, but they do not let it ruin their blossoming friendship.
Plot	Why does the Fury come to dinner at Bruno's house?	What impact does the dinner with the Fury have on Bruno's life?	The Fury invites himself to dinner at Bruno's house. He wants to discuss Father's military promotion and his new assignment at Out-With. At the dinner, Bruno realizes that he does not like the Fury or the way he treats people. After the dinner, Bruno's family moves from Berlin to Out-With, which makes Bruno very unhappy.

Name _____

Date _____

◼ Analyzing the Literature

Directions: Think about the section you just read. Read each question and state your response with textual evidence.

1. Why does Bruno's family argue on Christmas day?

   _____

   _____

   _____

   _____

2. Why does Bruno decide to explore outside at Out-With instead of inside like in Berlin?

   _____

   _____

   _____

   _____

3. Use the text to describe Shmuel.

   _____

   _____

   _____

   _____

4. Why does the Fury come to dinner at Bruno's house?

   _____

   _____

   _____

   _____

Name _____

Date _____

▲ Analyzing the Literature

Directions: Think about the section you just read. Read each question and state your response with textual evidence.

1. How does the argument on Christmas illustrate differing opinions in Germany at the time?

_____

_____

_____

_____

2. Why is Bruno so curious about the fence and the people who live behind it?

_____

_____

_____

_____

3. Compare and contrast Bruno and Shmuel.

_____

_____

_____

_____

4. What impact does the dinner with the Fury have on Bruno's life?

_____

_____

_____

_____

Name _____

Date _____

Reader Response

Directions: Choose one of the following prompts about this section to answer. Be sure you include a topic sentence in your response, use textual evidence to support your opinion, and provide a strong conclusion that summarizes your opinion.

Writing Prompts

- **Opinion/Argument Piece**—Father feels he is being a patriot to his country by following its leader, but Grandmother feels ashamed of him because of the terrible things he is supporting. Do you think it is more important to follow the government or your conscience?
- **Narrative Piece**—What predictions can you make about Bruno and Shmuel's friendship? Include examples from the text in your writing.

_____

_____

_____

_____

_____

_____

_____

_____

_____

_____

_____

_____

_____

_____

Name _____

Date _____

Close Reading the Literature

Directions: Closely reread the section in chapter 10 where Bruno and Shmuel discuss their homes. Begin when Shmuel says, "Where did you come from?" Stop when Bruno says, "Well, we'll have to agree to disagree." Read each question below and then revisit the text to find evidence that supports your answer.

1. Use details from the text to explain why Bruno will pay better attention during his geography lessons.

   _____

   _____

   _____

2. Do you think this section shows that Bruno is prejudiced? Use examples from the text to support your answer.

   _____

   _____

   _____

3. What does the author want you to infer from Bruno's statements about the changes in Berlin?

   _____

   _____

4. Why does Bruno suggest they "agree to disagree" about their homes? Use evidence from the section in your answer.

   _____

   _____

   _____

Name _____

Date _____

Making Connections—European Geography

Directions: Bruno and Shmuel are both unsure about their surrounding geography. Look at the map of Europe below and answer the questions.

1. List at least five countries that border Germany.

   _____

   _____

   _____

2. What two bodies of water border Germany?

   _____

3. Describe the locations of Denmark and Poland in relation to Germany.

   _____

   _____

Name _____

Date _____

Creating with the Story Elements

Directions: Thinking about the story elements of character, setting, and plot in a novel is very important to understanding what is happening and why. Complete **one** of the following activities based on what you've read so far. Be creative and have fun!

Characters

Make a KWL chart about Shmuel. In the first column, write three things you **know** about him; in the second column, write three things you **want** to find out. After you finish the book, come back to your chart and write what you **learned** about him.

Setting

Plan the dinner party at Bruno's home with the Fury and his beautiful blonde companion. Include an invitation, menu, and entertainment.

Plot

Reread Mother and Father's fragmented argument at the end of chapter 11. Rewrite the dialogue and add in what could be missing from their conversation.

Vocabulary Overview

Ten key words from this section are provided below with definitions and sentences about how the words are used in the book. Choose one of the vocabulary activity sheets (pages 45 or 46) for students to complete as they read this section. Monitor students as they work to ensure the definitions they have found are accurate and relate to the text. Finally, discuss these important vocabulary words with students. If you think these words or other words in the section warrant more time devoted to them, there are suggestions in the introduction for other vocabulary activities (page 5).

Word	Definition	Sentence about Text
contradict (ch. 12)	declare the opposite of what someone else has said	Bruno, thinking Shmuel's story does not make sense, opens his mouth to **contradict** him.
departing (ch. 12)	leaving	As Shmuel is **departing**, Bruno shouts to him.
catastrophe (ch. 13)	a terrible disaster	Bruno sees that something is wrong with Pavel and anxiously waits for **catastrophe** to strike.
incumbent (ch. 13)	necessary as a duty	Father says it is **incumbent** for everyone to play their part to help Germany.
revival (ch. 13)	becoming stronger, greater or more popular again	Father thinks there is going to be a national **revival** of Germany's glory.
ginger (ch. 13)	a fair-skinned person with red hair and freckles	Bruno cannot remember much about his friends in Berlin, except that one was a **ginger**.
dilemma (ch. 14)	a situation where a difficult choice must be made	Bruno finds himself in a **dilemma**, deciding whether or not to tell Gretel about Shmuel.
undeniable (ch. 14)	true and unable to be argued	The fact that Shmuel is Bruno's friend is **undeniable**.
seething (ch. 15)	full of unexpressed, intense emotion, especially anger	After Lieutenant Kotler teases him, Bruno is **seething** with anger.
grimaced (ch. 15)	a facial expression showing pain or disgust	When Bruno sees the bruising on Shmuel's face, he **grimaces** and forgets what he is saying.

Name _____

Date _____

Understanding Vocabulary Words

Directions: The following words appear in this section of the book. Use context clues and reference materials to determine an accurate definition for each word.

Word	Definition
contradict (ch. 12)	
departing (ch. 12)	
catastrophe (ch. 13)	
incumbent (ch. 13)	
revival (ch. 13)	
ginger (ch. 13)	
dilemma (ch. 14)	
undeniable (ch. 14)	
seething (ch. 15)	
grimaced (ch. 15)	

Name _____

Date _____

During-Reading Vocabulary Activity

Directions: As you read these chapters, record at least eight important words on the lines below. Try to find interesting, difficult, intriguing, special, or funny words. Your words can be long or short. They can be hard or easy to spell. After each word, use context clues in the text and reference materials to define the word.

- _____

- _____

- _____

- _____

- _____

- _____

- _____

- _____

- _____

- _____

Directions: Respond to these questions about the words in this section.

1. Why does Bruno want to **contradict** Shmuel?

_____

_____

2. What **catastrophe** happens to Pavel during dinner?

_____

_____

Analyzing the Literature

Provided below are discussion questions you can use in small groups, with the whole class, or for written assignments. Each question is given at two levels so you can choose the right question for each group of students. Activity sheets with these questions are provided (pages 48–49) if you want students to write their responses. For each question, a few key discussion points are provided for your reference.

Story Element	■ Level 1	▲ Level 2	Key Discussion Points
Setting	What changes happen to Shmuel and his family before they are brought to Out-With?	How are the experiences that brought Shmuel to Out-With different from the ones that brought Bruno there?	Shmuel and his family lived in the flat above their watch shop. First, everyone had to wear an armband with a star on it; then they had to move to one side of a big wall and live in one room with another family. They were loaded on a train to Out-With. Bruno's family came to the camp as part of his father's promotion. They rode a spacious train, and he lives in a house with plenty of food and space.
Plot	What does Lieutenant Kotler accidentally admit during dinner?	Why does Lieutenant Kotler feel uncomfortable after telling Father about his own father?	Lieutenant Kotler accidentally admits that his father left Germany for Switzerland. Father begins questioning the loyalty of Lieutenant Kotler's father, asking whether he might have had disagreements with government policy. Lieutenant Kotler is worried that he might lose status or face consequences because of his father.
Character	What stories does Bruno tell Gretel about Shmuel?	As Bruno shares stories about Shmuel with Gretel, what does he realize?	Bruno tells Gretel that Shmuel's friends disappeared without telling him good-bye and that Shmuel's grandfather has been missing for days. As Bruno shares the stories out loud, he realizes how sad Shmuel is about them. He becomes conscious of how insensitive he has been by switching the topic to silly things and promises himself he will apologize.
Plot	How does Bruno betray Shmuel in the kitchen?	Why does Bruno betray Shmuel in the kitchen?	Shmuel says Bruno gave him the food and that they are friends. Bruno denies this and says he has never seen or spoken to Shmuel before. Bruno betrays Shmuel because he is very afraid of Lieutenant Kotler. Bruno remembers what Kotler did to Pavel and how he shot the dog. Bruno knows he will be in trouble if he admits his friendship with Shmuel, so he denies it.

Name _____

Date _____

◼ Analyzing the Literature

Directions: Think about the section you just read. Read each question and state your response with textual evidence.

1. What changes happen to Shmuel and his family before they are brought to Out-With?

    _____

    _____

    _____

    _____

2. What does Lieutenant Kotler accidentally admit during dinner?

    _____

    _____

    _____

    _____

3. What stories does Bruno tell Gretel about Shmuel?

    _____

    _____

    _____

    _____

4. How does Bruno betray Shmuel in the kitchen?

    _____

    _____

    _____

    _____

Name _____

Date _____

▲ Analyzing the Literature

Directions: Think about the section you just read. Read each question and state your response with textual evidence.

1. How are the experiences that brought Shmuel to Out-With different from the ones that brought Bruno there?

_____

_____

_____

_____

2. Why does Lieutenant Kotler feel uncomfortable after telling Father about his own father?

_____

_____

_____

_____

3. As Bruno shares stories about Shmuel with Gretel, what does he realize?

_____

_____

_____

_____

4. Why does Bruno betray Shmuel in the kitchen?

_____

_____

_____

_____

Name _____

Date _____

Reader Response

Directions: Choose one of the following prompts about this section to answer. Be sure you include a topic sentence in your response, use textual evidence to support your opinion, and provide a strong conclusion that summarizes your opinion.

Writing Prompts

- **Opinion/Argument Piece**—When Bruno is asked if he knows Shmuel, he denies their friendship. Do you think he did the right thing? Use information from the text and any personal experiences to support your opinion.

- **Informative/Explanatory Piece**—"The only thing necessary for the triumph of evil is that good men do nothing" is a famous quotation attributed to Edmund Burke. How do these words relate to what happens to Pavel during dinner with Lieutenant Kotler?

_____

_____

_____

_____

_____

_____

_____

_____

_____

_____

_____

_____

_____

Name _____

Date _____

Close Reading the Literature

Directions: Closely reread the section in chapter 13 where Bruno and Shmuel discuss soldiers. Begin when Bruno asks, "Do you know what you want to be when you grow up?" Continue until he says, "The evenings *are* getting chillier." Read each question below and then revisit the text to find evidence that supports your answer.

1. According to Bruno, what makes a man a good soldier?

   _____

   _____

2. Why, as stated in the text, does Bruno change the subject after Shmuel says, "You don't know what it's like here"?

   _____

   _____

   _____

3. How does Gretel behave around Lieutenant Kotler? Use examples from this section to tell what this shows about their relationship.

   _____

   _____

   _____

4. Both Bruno and Shmuel are afraid of Lieutenant Kotler. Use inferencing and text support to explain why they are each afraid of him.

   _____

   _____

   _____

Name

Date

Making Connections—Cultural Symbols

Directions: Look at each religious or cultural symbol on the left. Read the descriptions on the right. Put the letter of the correct description in the box next to the symbol it matches.

1. Star of David	☐	**A.** represents a sacred sound in Hindu and is used for meditation; made up of three Sanskrit letters
2. Aum	☐	**B.** symbolizes the crucifixion of Jesus Christ, the man on whose life Christianity is founded
3. Yin Yang	☐	**C.** Buddhist symbol called the "Wheel of the Law;" has eight spokes which represent the eightfold path
4. Cross	☐	**D.** symbol of Judaism with unknown origins; some people think the upward triangle represents God and the downward triangle represents people on Earth
5. Dharmachakra	☐	**E.** often indicates Islam on flags or logos, although Islamic people do not believe in holy symbols
6. Crescent and Star	☐	**F.** Chinese symbol of balance; the two parts represent opposites such as positive and negative or male and female

Name _____

Date _____

Creating with the Story Elements

Directions: Thinking about the story elements of character, setting, and plot in a novel is very important to understanding what is happening and why. Complete **one** of the following activities based on what you've read so far. Be creative and have fun!

Characters

Maria says she will tell Bruno all she knows about Pavel, but this conversation is not included in the book. Write the story she might have shared with Bruno about Pavel. Use information from the book and your imagination.

Setting

Shmuel tells Bruno the story of how he went from living above his Papa's watch shop to living at Out-With. Draw a picture for each part of his journey.

Plot

Pretend Bruno did tell Lieutenant Kotler about his friendship with Shmuel when challenged in the kitchen. Make a list of at least five things that might have happened as a result of his confession.

Vocabulary Overview

Ten key words from this section are provided below with definitions and sentences about how the words are used in the book. Choose one of the vocabulary activity sheets (pages 55 or 56) for students to complete as they read this section. Monitor students as they work to ensure the definitions they have found are accurate and relate to the text. Finally, discuss these important vocabulary words with students. If you think these words or other words in the section warrant more time devoted to them, there are suggestions in the introduction for other vocabulary activities (page 5).

Word	Definition	Sentence about Text
starched (ch. 16)	stiffened with a spray before ironing	Father wears his **starched** and pressed uniform at Grandmother's funeral.
inconsolable (ch. 16)	not able to be comforted	Gretel is **inconsolable** when Lieutenant Kotler is sent away from Out-With.
dwindling (ch. 16)	gradually getting smaller in size or amount	Bruno's finds that his self-confidence is **dwindling** after his head is shaved.
senile (ch. 17)	losing mental ability in old age	Father says Grandfather no longer writes to the family because he has gone **senile**.
summon (ch. 17)	to ask a person to come to a meeting	Father wants to speak with Bruno and Gretel and **summons** them to his office.
smuggled (ch. 18)	secretly brought something from one place to another	Bruno gives the bread and apple he **smuggled** out of the house to Shmuel.
coincidences (ch. 18)	events that are the same or happen at the same time, without being planned	Bruno knows that **coincidences** can happen, such as he and Shmuel having the same birthday.
conceded (ch. 18)	admitted that something was true when at first you said it wasn't	Shmuel **concedes** that he and Bruno look much alike since Bruno got his hair cut.
prospect (ch. 19)	the possibility that something will happen	Finding Shmuel's Papa is not as exciting a **prospect** to Bruno as the prospect of exploring.
mercilessly (ch. 20)	showing no kindness	Father treats the soldiers at Out-With **mercilessly** and becomes very unpopular.

Name _____

Date _____

Understanding Vocabulary Words

Directions: The following words appear in this section of the book. Use context clues and reference materials to determine an accurate definition for each word.

Word	Definition
starched (ch. 16)	
inconsolable (ch. 16)	
dwindling (ch. 16)	
senile (ch. 17)	
summoned (ch. 17)	
smuggled (ch. 18)	
coincidences (ch. 18)	
conceded (ch. 18)	
prospect (ch. 19)	
mercilessly (ch. 20)	

Name

Date

During-Reading Vocabulary Activity

Directions: As you read these chapters, choose five important words from the story. Then, use those five words to complete this word flow chart. On each arrow, write a vocabulary word. In the boxes between the words, explain how the words connect. An example for the words *forlorn* and *dwindling* has been done for you.

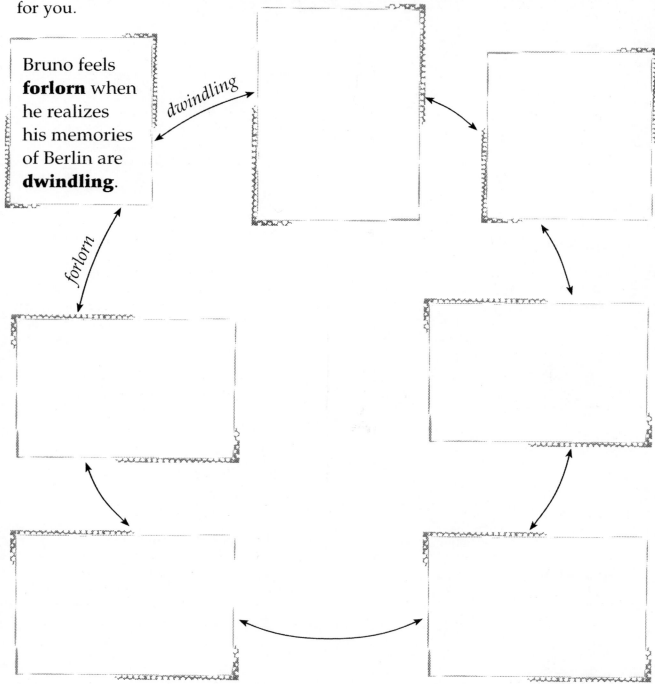

Bruno feels **forlorn** when he realizes his memories of Berlin are **dwindling**.

dwindling

forlorn

Analyzing the Literature

Provided below are discussion questions you can use in small groups, with the whole class, or for written assignments. Each question is given at two levels so you can choose the right question for each group of students. Activity sheets with these questions are provided (pages 58–59) if you want students to write their responses. For each question, a few key discussion points are provided for your reference.

Story Element	■ Level 1	▲ Level 2	Key Discussion Points
Character	What happens to Lieutenant Kotler?	Why is Lieutenant Kotler transferred?	Lieutenant Kotler is sent away from Out-With. The text does not explicitly say why he is transferred, but readers may infer that it is because of the information he shares about his father during dinner. Another theory may be that he is developing a relationship with either Bruno's mother or with Gretel that Father does not like.
Setting	Why does Bruno want to visit Shmuel's side of the fence?	Compare and contrast the reasons Bruno and Shmuel have for wanting Bruno to visit Shmuel's side of the fence.	Bruno wants to visit because he is leaving Out-With and returning to Berlin. He and Shmuel never got to play together. Both boys want to spend time together since Bruno is leaving. Bruno wants to explore and see how Shmuel lives while Shmuel wants help to find his Papa.
Plot	Why is Bruno able to walk around undetected at Out-With with Shmuel?	What precautions do Bruno and Shmuel take so Bruno can visit the camp without being detected?	Bruno can walk around with Shmuel because he resembles the other children at Out-With. Like them, he is male. His head is shaved because he had lice. Shmuel brings Bruno an extra pair of striped pajamas and a cap to wear and convinces him to leave his shoes behind and go barefoot.
Plot	Do you think Father figures out what happened to Bruno? Why?	How do you know that Father eventually figures out what happened to Bruno?	Father appears to figure out that Bruno went inside the camp and was killed there. The text says Father goes to the spot where Bruno's clothes were found, notices the weak spot in the fence, follows the steps logically, and then collapses. The reader may presume that he is overwhelmed with the realization of what happened to Bruno.

Name _____

Date _____

■ Analyzing the Literature

Directions: Think about the section you just read. Read each question and state your response with textual evidence.

1. What happens to Lieutenant Kotler?

_____

_____

_____

_____

2. Why does Bruno want to visit Shmuel's side of the fence?

_____

_____

_____

_____

3. Why is Bruno able to walk around undetected at Out-With with Shmuel?

_____

_____

_____

_____

4. Do you think Father figures out what happened to Bruno? Why?

_____

_____

_____

_____

Name _____

Date _____

▲ Analyzing the Literature

Directions: Think about the section you just read. Read each question and state your response with textual evidence.

1. Why is Lieutenant Kotler transferred?

_____

_____

_____

_____

2. Compare and contrast the reasons Bruno and Shmuel have for wanting Bruno to visit Shmuel's side of the fence.

_____

_____

_____

_____

3. What precautions do Bruno and Shmuel take so Bruno can visit the camp without being detected?

_____

_____

_____

_____

4. How do you know that Father eventually figures out what happened to Bruno?

_____

_____

_____

Name _____

Date _____

Reader Response

Directions: Choose one of the following prompts about this section to answer. Be sure you include a topic sentence in your response, use textual evidence to support your opinion, and provide a strong conclusion that summarizes your opinion.

Writing Prompts

- **Opinion/Argument Piece**—Author John Boyne uses the names "Out-With" and "the Fury" instead of Auschwitz and the Führer (Hitler) for the entire book. Why do you think he made that choice and what effect does it have on the story?

- **Informative/Explanatory Piece**—Bruno's fate is a result of several events in the story. What are these events and how do they lead to his death?

_____

_____

_____

_____

_____

_____

_____

_____

_____

_____

_____

_____

_____

_____

Name _____

Date _____

Close Reading the Literature

Directions: Closely reread Gretel and Bruno's conversation about the fence in chapter 16. Begin with, "Gretel's room had changed quite considerably since the last time he had been there." Stop when Bruno says, "Well, can't someone just get them together and—" Read each question below and then revisit the text to find evidence that supports your answer.

1. How has Gretel's room changed? What does this show about changes in her character as well?

   _____

   _____

   _____

2. Use examples from the section to show Bruno is naïve.

   _____

   _____

   _____

3. Is Gretel sharing her actual beliefs with Bruno, or is she repeating what she has heard? Use inferencing to explain your answer.

   _____

   _____

   _____

4. What do you think the author wants people to understand about prejudice in this section? How do you know this from the text?

   _____

   _____

Name _____

Date _____

Making Connections–Remembering the Holocaust

Directions: Read the paragraphs below. Then, answer the questions.

Since the end of World War II in 1945, more than 25 countries have built memorials to the Holocaust. The United States Holocaust Memorial Museum (USHMM) opened on April 22, 1993, in Washington, D.C. More than 30 million people have visited the museum since it opened.

The permanent exhibit is called *The Holocaust*. It covers three floors, each focusing on a part of the Holocaust's history. The first floor, *Nazi Assault*, is about the rise of the Nazi party before World War II. Next, *Final Solution* teaches visitors about the wartime treatment of Jews. Finally, *Last Chapter* shows the Allied victory and what happened after the Holocaust.

Remember the Children: Daniel's Story is an exhibit aimed at children eight and older. People can walk through the life of a fictional boy named Daniel. It starts at his home where visitors can visit his kitchen and bedroom. Then visitors visit the ghetto, where many Jewish people were forced to move. Following time on the train, visitors end up at a concentration camp. At the end of the tour, children can write their thoughts or draw pictures and put them on a big bulletin board to share with other visitors.

1. Why do you think people build memorials to the Holocaust?

   _____

   _____

2. Which exhibit would you choose to view? Give at least two reasons.

   _____

   _____

   _____

3. Why would the museum choose to build an exhibit especially for children?

   _____

   _____

Name _____

Date _____

Creating with the Story Elements

Directions: Thinking about the story elements of character, setting, and plot in a novel is very important to understanding what is happening and why. Complete **one** of the following activities based on what you've read so far. Be creative and have fun!

Characters

Make a list of at least five ways Bruno changes during the book.

Setting

Until Bruno goes inside Out-With with Shmuel, he does not really understand what it is like. Draw a picture of Bruno's original idea of Out-With. Then, draw a picture of what he sees during his visit. Use the text and your imagination.

Plot

Pretend you are one of the soldiers collecting evidence after Bruno's disappearance. Plan your investigation. Make a list of questions to ask witnesses and townspeople. Formulate some theories as to why Bruno's clothes are found by the fence.

Name _____

Date _____

Post-Reading Theme Thoughts

Directions: Read each of the statements in the first column. Choose a main character from *The Boy in the Striped Pajamas*. Think about that character's point of view. From that character's perspective, decide if the character would agree or disagree with the statements. Record the character's opinion by marking an X in Agree or Disagree for each statement. Explain your choices in the fourth column using text evidence.

Character I Chose: _____

Statement	Agree	Disagree	Explain Your Answer
It is best to protect children from knowing about difficult things.			
A person should always support his or her family members.			
If a person is doing something wrong, he or she knows it.			
People who are very different can be friends.			

Culminating Activity: Book Review

Overview: Reading a review is helpful to people who are interested in a book. However, it can also be helpful to the person who writes the review! When a person writes a review, he or she must think deeply about the characters and plot, form and defend opinions, and persuade others to feel the same.

Directions: Think about the questions listed below. Then, write your thoughts about the book.

- What do you really like or enjoy about the book?
- Is there anything you do not like or agree with?
- What do you think of the characters?
- Would you change anything if you were the author?
- How does the book make you feel?
- Does the book teach you anything?
- Who do you think would enjoy reading this book?

_____

_____

_____

_____

_____

_____

_____

_____

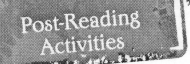
Name _____

Date _____

Culminating Activity: Book Review (cont.)

Directions: When you have completed writing your thoughts about the novel, choose one type of review below to create. Your review should thoughtfully express your feelings and opinions about the book. Be creative and have fun! If class time allows, share your review with your classmates!

Written

This traditional type of review should be typed. After you finish your final copy, upload your review to a classroom website, blog, or even a commercial website like Amazon.com.

Audio

Record your voice to create a podcast review. Adding expression to your voice and using sound effects will add interest for your listeners.

Video

Get out your camera to record a video review. You could use acting, props, or visual aids to grab your audience's attention.

Name

Date

Comprehension Assessment

Directions: Circle the letter for the best response to each question.

1. What is the meaning of "the Fury" as used in the book?

    A. the leader of the Nazi German government

    B. Bruno's nickname for his sister, Gretel

    C. Lieutenant Kotler's temper

    D. Mother's feelings about Out-With

2. Which detail from the book best supports your answer to question 1?

    E. "Lieutenant Kotler grew very angry with Pavel and no one . . . stepped in to stop him doing what he did next . . . ."

    F. "he [Father] was a man to watch and that the Fury had big things in mind for him."

    G. "It's horrible . . . Just horrible. I can't stand it any more."

    H. "if anyone was the Hopeless Case around here, it wasn't him."

3. What is the main idea of the text below?

    "'When did you arrive at Out-With?' asked Bruno."

    "Pavel put the carrot and the peeler down for a few moments and thought about it. 'I think I've always been here,' he said finally in a quiet voice.

    "'You grew up here?'

    "No,' Pavel said, shaking his head. 'No, I didn't.'"

    _____

    _____

    _____

4. Choose **two** details from those below to support your answer to number 3.

    A. Maria enjoys the gardens at the house in Berlin.

    B. Shmuel's mother makes armbands with a star for his family to wear.

    C. Pavel gently cleans and bandages Bruno's wound.

    D. Shmuel's family is forced to move and has to live with another family in one room.

Comprehension Assessment (cont.)

5. Which statement best expresses a theme of the book?

    A. It is hard to overcome differences.

    B. People cannot always find a way to get along.

    C. Following the rules is necessary.

    D. Friendship is important, especially in bad times.

6. What detail from the book provides the best evidence for your answer to number 5?

    E. "I suppose that's what I'm doing, isn't it? Pretending to be a person from the other side of the fence."

    F. "The fence isn't there to stop us from going over there. It's to stop them from coming over here."

    G. "It makes me so proud to see you elevated to such a responsible position."

    H. ". . . he took hold of Shmuel's tiny hand in his and squeezed it tightly."

7. What is the purpose of these sentences from the book: "'Ah, those people,' said Father, nodding his head and smiling slightly. 'Those people . . . well, they're not people at all, Bruno.'"

    _____

    _____

    _____

8. Which other quotation from the story serves a similar purpose?

    A. "This is my work, important work. Important to our country. Important to the Fury. You'll understand that some day."

    B. "I don't see why I have to be stuck over here in this side of the fence where there's no one to talk to and no one to play with . . . ."

    C. "That's why they have to be kept together. They can't mix with us."

    D. "'I've never spoken to him,' said Bruno immediately. 'I've never seen him before in my life. I don't know him.'"

Name _____

Date _____

Response to Literature: Modern-Day Fences

Overview: The fence in *The Boy in the Striped Pajamas* is an actual, physical thing that separates two friends based on politics and religion. Author John Boyne wrote, "Fences like this exist all over the world. We hope you never have to encounter one." Though they may not be able to be seen or touched, there are still "fences" left in the United States and the world. These dividing fences can be based on:

- Race (physical characteristics)
- Class (wealth or education)
- Gender (being male or female)

Directions: Select one of these invisible "fences" and do research to learn more about it. Where is the problem happening? What is the effect on the culture? Is anything being done to fight the injustice? If so, what? Write a researched essay showing your understanding of the chosen topic and compare and contrast it with the fence in the novel. Use facts and details about the topic, and also cite the novel to support your thinking. In conclusion, explain your opinion about this question: Will these types of "fences" ever disappear from society?

Your essay response to literature should follow these guidelines:

- Write at least 750 words.
- Include main points, such as those listed in the directions above.
- Provide a conclusion that summarizes your point of view.
- Final essays are due on _____

Name _____

Date _____

Response to Literature Rubric

Directions: Use this rubric to evaluate student responses.

	Exceptional Writing	Quality Writing	Developing Writing
Focus and Organization	☐ States a clear opinion and elaborates well. Engages the reader from the opening hook through the middle to the conclusion. Demonstrates clear understanding of the intended audience and purpose of the piece.	☐ Provides a clear and consistent opinion. Maintains a clear perspective and supports it through elaborating details. Makes the opinion clear in the opening hook and summarizes well in the conclusion.	☐ Provides an inconsistent point of view. Does not support the topic adequately or misses pertinent information. Provides lack of clarity in the beginning, middle, and conclusion.
Text Evidence	☐ Provides comprehensive and accurate support. Includes relevant and worthwhile text references.	☐ Provides limited support. Provides few supporting text references.	☐ Provides very limited support for the text. Provides no supporting text references.
Written Expression	☐ Uses descriptive and precise language with clarity and intention. Maintains a consistent voice and uses an appropriate tone that supports meaning. Uses multiple sentence types and transitions well between ideas.	☐ Uses a broad vocabulary. Maintains a consistent voice and supports a tone and feelings through language. Varies sentence length and word choices.	☐ Uses a limited and unvaried vocabulary. Provides an inconsistent or weak voice and tone. Provides little to no variation in sentence type and length.
Language Conventions	☐ Capitalizes, punctuates, and spells accurately. Demonstrates complete thoughts within sentences, with accurate subject-verb agreement. Uses paragraphs appropriately and with clear purpose.	☐ Capitalizes, punctuates, and spells accurately. Demonstrates complete thoughts within sentences and appropriate grammar. Paragraphs are properly divided and supported.	☐ Incorrectly capitalizes, punctuates, and spells. Uses fragmented or run-on sentences. Utilizes poor grammar overall. Paragraphs are poorly divided and developed.

The responses provided here are just examples of what students may answer. Many accurate responses are possible for the questions throughout this unit.

During-Reading Vocabulary Activity—Section 1:
Chapters 1–4 (page 16)

1. Bruno feels Maria's **priorities** should be unpacking his toys and books, not his clothing.

2. Gretel's view is **decidedly** better because she cannot see the fence or the camp from her window.

Close Reading the Literature—Section 1:
Chapters 1–4 (page 21)

1. Gretel suggests they are at the countryside because there is so much open space between the huts in the camp. She learned in school that farmers grow food on lots of land, and it is brought to the city for the people there to eat.

2. When Bruno disagrees with Gretel, she says, "You're *nine*." She tells Bruno that maybe he will understand things better when he is her age.

3. Bruno's argument is that he cannot see any farm animals. "There should be cows and pigs and sheep and horses." He also points out that the land is dry and dusty, not suitable for growing crops.

4. For a moment when he sits down, Bruno wishes that Gretel would put her arm around him and make him feel better about living at Out-With. However, Gretel is still preoccupied with the view out the window.

Making Connections—Section 1:
Chapters 1–4 (page 22)

1. two years

2. Japan bombed Pearl Harbor.

3. D-Day, Battle of the Bulge

4. Student responses will vary but may include: Countries join together so they can share troops, strategies, and supplies. Countries join together because they share a common view of what is right.

During-Reading Vocabulary Activity—Section 2
Chapters 5–7 (page 26)

1. Bruno feels **incredulous** because Maria tells him he cannot say what he feels.

2. Bruno should not laugh at Herr Roller's **escapades** because he received a head injury in the Great War and is not quite right anymore.

Close Reading the Literature—Section 2:
Chapters 5–7 (page 31)

1. Bruno is surprised to find out Pavel is a doctor because he does not have a prestigious position at Bruno's house. "But you're a waiter . . . And you peel the vegetables for dinner."

2. The misunderstanding over the word "practise" is that they are thinking of different definitions. Pavel means a doctor practises medicine, or does that as his living. Bruno is using the more common definition, to perform a skill repeatedly in hopes of getting better. Bruno thinks Pavel was not an accomplished doctor and was trying to improve.

3. An inference from Pavel's statement could be that although he hasn't physically been at Out-With his entire life, he has always felt prejudice and oppression because he is Jewish. Pavel's submissive demeanor, skinny build, and even his missing beard are clues that he has not been treated fairly for a long time.

4. When they hear Mother's voice, Pavel jumps up quickly from his seat and returns to the sink with his work, "hanging his head low and not speaking again."

Making Connections—Section 2:
Chapters 5–7 (page 32)

Sample instructions:

1. Gather materials such as a long piece of rope, a tire, scissors, and a ladder.

2. Tie the rope securely to a low, strong branch.

3. Tie the bottom of the rope to the tire.

4. Check for sturdiness.

Sample answer: Children should not build tire swings by themselves. It could be dangerous because the child would have to climb a tree, and a child could not test the swing's strength well enough.

Close Reading the Literature—Section 3:
Chapters 8–11 (page 41)

1. When Bruno is talking with Shmuel, he tries to sound clever by mentioning places like Germany, Poland, and Denmark. He gets them all confused, though, and starts to realize that he has things entirely wrong. He makes a "private resolution to pay more attention in the future in geography class."

2. Sample answers: Bruno is prejudiced because he says Germany is superior to Poland and that Germany is the best country of all. Bruno is not prejudiced because even though he says Germany is better than Poland, he feels uncomfortable saying it and does not want to sound unkind.

3. Bruno says Berlin "was much nicer before things changed." He mentions that the city became "noisy" and "scary" and that there are blackouts. We can infer that Bruno was not as happy in Berlin as he thought and that the war has brought uncomfortable changes to the city.

4. The boys each think his home is better. Bruno likes his house, the shops, and the cafés, while Shmuel says his home is very friendly and the food is better. Bruno "does not want to fight with his new friend," so he wants to agree to disagree.

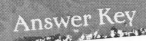

Making Connections—Section 3:
Chapter 8–11 (page 42)

1. Denmark, Poland, Czech Republic, Austria, Switzerland, France, Belgium, Netherlands

2. North Sea, Baltic Sea

3. Denmark is north of Germany. Poland is east of Germany.

During-Reading Vocabulary Activity—Section 4:
Chapters 12–15 (page 46)

1. Bruno wants to **contradict** Shmuel because Shmuel says he lived in one room with 11 people, and Bruno does not think that is possible.

2. Pavel's **catastrophe** is that he has trouble staying upright and fulfilling his duties at dinner and eventually spills a bottle of red wine on Lieutenant Kotler's lap.

Close Reading the Literature—Section 4:
Chapters 12–15 (page 51)

1. Bruno says a good soldier is one like Father who "has an impressive uniform and . . . everyone calls him Commandant and does whatever he says."

2. Bruno changes the subject "because then he wouldn't have to answer" or acknowledge Shmuel's difficult statement. Deep down, Bruno knows something very bad is going on at the camp, and he doesn't want to deal with it or accept that his father would be a part of it.

3. Bruno says Gretel and Lieutenant Kotler are always laughing together and she waits for him to come to the house. When she sees him, she pretends it was an accident that that they ran into each other. They have a flirtatious relationship, which may not be appropriate as he is much older and a soldier.

4. The text says Bruno is afraid of Lieutenant Kotler because he is a bully and wears too much cologne. We can infer that Shmuel is afraid of him because he is cruel and abusive to the people at Out-With.

Making Connections—Section 4:
Chapters 12–15 (page 52)

1. D.
2. A.
3. F.
4. B.
5. C.
6. E.

Close Reading the Literature—Section 5:
Chapters 16–20 (page 61)

1. The text says Gretel's dolls are gone and the walls are filled with maps. She spends hours reading the paper and moving pins from one place to another on the maps. Gretel is growing up and maturing; the childish dolls are no longer entertaining to her and the world outside her own experience is much more interesting.

2. Bruno continues to mispronounce the name of the camp and does not realize he is saying it incorrectly, even when his mistake is directly pointed out. He thinks the fence is there to keep him out; he does not realize it is to keep the people on the other side enclosed. He also has never heard the word "Jews."

3. We can infer Gretel is just repeating what she has heard. She is insulted when Bruno asks if they are Jews, but she does not know why that word is insulting. Though she knows the fence is to keep Jews away from people like her family, she does not know why the two groups should be separated or even what non-Jews should be called.

4. The author wants us to understand that prejudice often comes from not knowing or understanding something. Also that people are easily influenced by others and will adopt their opinions. In the text, Gretel shows prejudice towards the Jews, but she has no reason to support her feelings and cannot explain why Jews should be treated differently.

Comprehension Assessment (pages 67–68)

1. A. the leader of the Nazi German government

2. F. "he [Father] was a man to watch and that the Fury had big things in mind for him."

3. Main Idea: Prejudice against the Jews existed before Out-With was built. He has dealt with prejudice his whole life.

4. B. Shmuel's mother makes armbands with a star for his family to wear.

   D. Shmuel's family is forced to move and has to live with another family in one room.

5. D. Friendship is important, especially in bad times.

6. H. ". . . he took hold of Shmuel's tiny hand in his and squeezed it tightly."

7. These sentences show how deeply the prejudice was felt by Nazi Germany. The Jewish people were not merely considered lesser humans, but they were thought not to be people at all. This may be one way of understanding how Father, who previously in his life showed himself to be a compassionate person, is now able to take a job in such a terrible place.

8. C. "That's why they have to be kept together. They can't mix with us."